DEADLIEST ANIMALS

TAIPAN

BY RACHEL HAMBY

WWW.APEXEDITIONS.COM

Apex is distributed by North Star Editions:
sales@northstareditions.com | 888-417-0195

Produced for Apex by Red Line Editorial.

Photographs ©: Shutterstock Images, cover, 1, 4–5, 6, 8–9, 10–11, 12, 13, 14–15, 16–17, 18, 20, 22–23, 25, 29; iStockphoto, 6–7, 19, 24, 26–27

Library of Congress Control Number: 2022901417

ISBN
978-1-63738-288-2 (hardcover)
978-1-63738-324-7 (paperback)
978-1-63738-395-7 (ebook pdf)
978-1-63738-360-5 (hosted ebook)

Printed in the United States of America
Mankato, MN
082022

NOTE TO PARENTS AND EDUCATORS

Apex books are designed to build literacy skills in striving readers. Exciting, high-interest content attracts and holds readers' attention. The text is carefully leveled to allow students to achieve success quickly. Additional features, such as bolded glossary words for difficult terms, help build comprehension.

TABLE OF CONTENTS

CHAPTER 1

A DEADLY BITE 4

CHAPTER 2

LIFE IN THE WILD 10

CHAPTER 3

TAIPAN BODIES 16

CHAPTER 4

HUNTING AND EATING 22

COMPREHENSION QUESTIONS • 28

GLOSSARY • 30

TO LEARN MORE • 31

ABOUT THE AUTHOR • 31

INDEX • 32

A DEADLY BITE

A taipan slithers along the ground. It is hunting for **prey**. The snake raises its head. It spots a rat.

Taipans have good eyesight. This helps them find food.

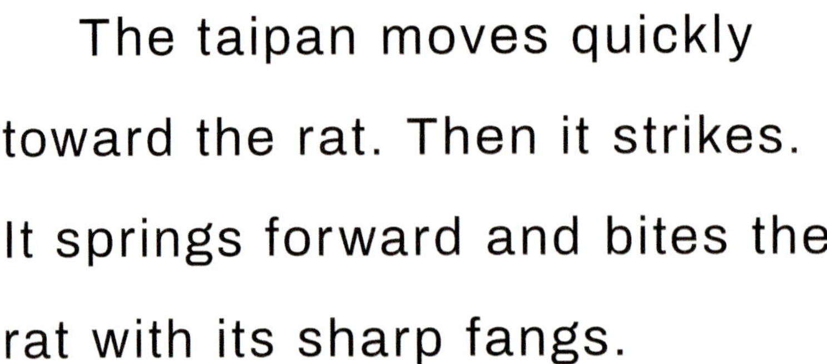

The taipan moves quickly toward the rat. Then it strikes. It springs forward and bites the rat with its sharp fangs.

Taipans mainly eat long-haired rats.

Taipans show their fangs when they hunt and when they sense danger.

FAST FACT

Taipans often kill their prey with many quick bites.

Taipans have long, forked tongues.

Poison flows through the taipan's fangs. It kills the rat. Then the taipan eats the rat. It swallows the rat whole.

STRONG SENSES

Taipans use both sight and smell to hunt. To smell, snakes flick their tongues in and out of their mouths. They pick up scents from the air. The snakes follow these scents to find prey.

CHAPTER 2

LIFE IN THE WILD

There are three different **species** of taipans. These snakes are found in Australia and New Guinea. Some live in forests. Others live in **deserts**.

The inland taipan lives in central Australia. Land there is dry and hot.

Taipans usually live alone. But males and females pair up to **mate**. Female taipans lay eggs. The eggs hatch two or three months later.

A taipan's eggs have soft sides.

Male taipans are usually bigger than female taipans.

FIGHTING TAIPANS

Male taipans fight over females. Two males curl around each other. One snake tries to push down the other snake's head. The snake that wins the fight mates with the female.

The baby snakes live on their own. They grow quickly. After one year, they can be 3 feet (1 m) long.

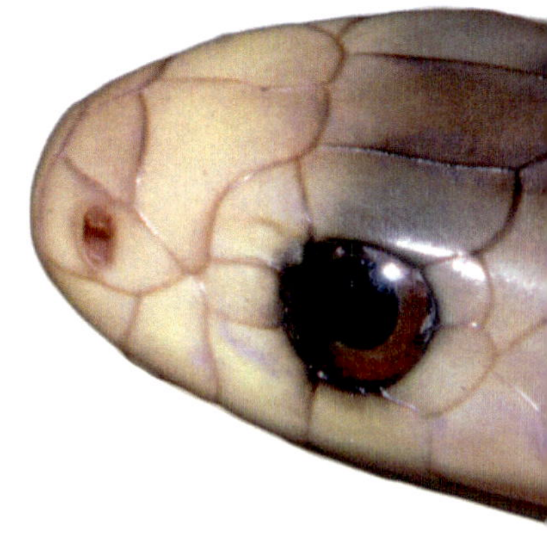

Baby taipans start hunting right after they hatch.

CHAPTER 3

TAIPAN BODIES

Taipans are large snakes. They can grow more than 8 feet (2 m) long. Their bodies are covered in hard scales.

Coastal taipans are the biggest type. They can be 9.5 feet (3 m) long.

Like all snakes, taipans are **reptiles**. All reptiles are **cold-blooded**. Their bodies take in heat from the sun. So, they usually live in warm places.

Some taipans can live to be 15 years old.

FAST FACT

An adult coastal taipan's scales get darker during cooler months. This helps the snake soak up more sunlight.

Taipans lie in the sun to warm their bodies.

Taipans often curl their bodies into an S-shape before they bite.

Taipans have strong muscles. They can move quickly. And they can jump high off the ground. This helps them catch birds and other prey.

HOW SNAKES MOVE

A snake uses its muscles to slither. The snake makes S-shaped movements. It pushes down where its body curves. The scales on its belly grip the ground.

CHAPTER 4

HUNTING AND EATING

Taipans usually hunt in the morning. They mainly eat rats and mice. First, they trap their prey. Then, they strike.

Coastal taipans sometimes eat lizards and birds.

Coastal taipans are less poisonous than inland taipans. But they are still dangerous.

A taipan's poison quickly kills the prey. The animal's muscles stop working. It can't breathe. Its heart stops beating.

THE INLAND TAIPAN

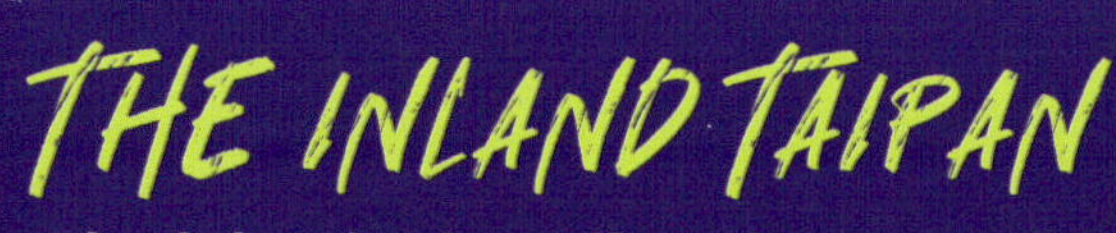

The inland taipan lives in Australia. It is the world's deadliest snake. Its poison can kill a human. This snake usually hides from people. But it will attack if it feels threatened.

Only a few people have been bitten by inland taipans.

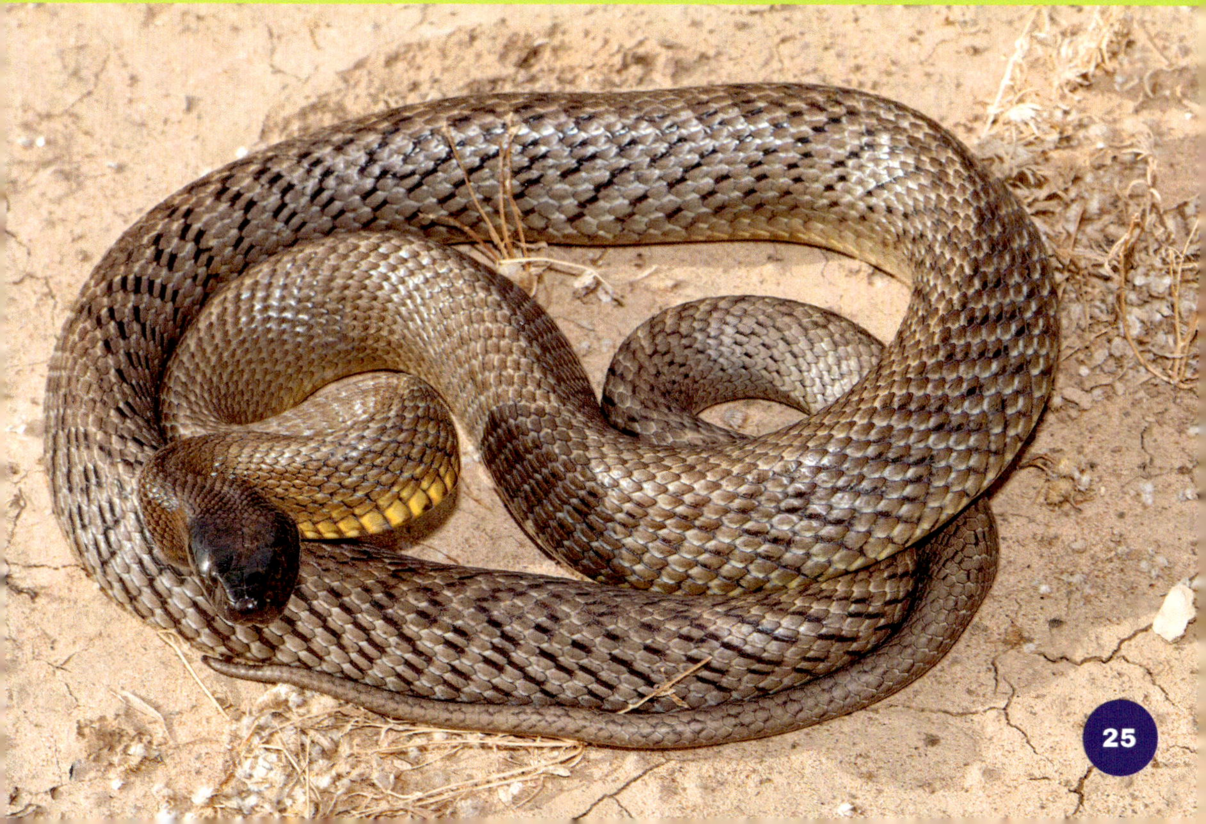

Taipans rest in the sun after eating.

To eat its prey, a taipan stretches its jaws wide. The snake's ribs and skin stretch, too. They expand to let the snake swallow large prey.

COMPREHENSION QUESTIONS

Write your answers on a separate piece of paper.

1. Write a few sentences describing how a taipan hunts prey.

2. Which of a taipan's abilities do you find most impressive? Why?

3. What part of its body does a taipan use to smell?

- **A.** its scales
- **B.** its tongue
- **C.** its fangs

4. Why do female taipans hide their eggs?

- **A.** to make it harder for lizards or birds to eat them
- **B.** to keep male taipans from finding them
- **C.** to keep the eggs from hatching

5. What does **deadliest** mean in this book?

It is the world's deadliest snake. Its poison can kill a human.

A. most likely to run away
B. most likely to be eaten
C. most likely to kill

6. What does **expand** mean in this book?

The snake's ribs and skin stretch, too. They expand to let the snake swallow large prey.

A. to get bigger
B. to get smaller
C. to change color

Answer key on page 32.

GLOSSARY

cold-blooded
Having a body temperature that matches the temperature of the surrounding water or air.

deserts
Areas of land that have few plants and get very little rain.

mate
To form a pair and come together to have babies.

prey
An animal that is hunted and eaten by another animal.

reptiles
Cold-blooded animals that have scales.

scents
Smells left behind by an animal.

species
Groups of animals or plants that are similar and can breed with one another.

threatened
Put in danger.

BOOKS

Holmes, Parker. *Pythons on the Hunt*. Minneapolis: Lerner Publications, 2018.

Jackson, Tom. *World's Deadliest Reptiles*. Minneapolis: Hungry Tomato, 2019.

Santos, Tracie. *Snakes and Other Reptiles*. Vero Beach, FL: Rourke Educational Media, 2021.

ONLINE RESOURCES

Visit www.apexeditions.com to find links and resources related to this title.

ABOUT THE AUTHOR

Rachel Hamby writes poetry, fiction, and nonfiction for young readers. She lives in Washington State with her husband, kids, and corgis.

INDEX

A

Australia, 10, 25

C

coastal taipan, 19

E

eating, 8, 27
eggs, 12, 14

F

fangs, 6
fighting, 13

H

hunting, 4–6, 9, 21–22

I

inland taipan, 25

M

mating, 12–13

N

New Guinea, 10

P

poison, 8, 24–25
prey, 4–9, 22–24, 27

R

reptiles, 18

S

scales, 16
slithering, 4, 21
smelling, 9

ANSWER KEY:

1. Answers will vary; 2. Answers will vary; 3. B; 4. A; 5. C; 6. A